Faith WEBBING

Wrapping Children and Youth in a Web of Faith

GARY M. PECUCH

Faith Webbing
Wrapping Children and Youth in a Web of Faith
by Gary M. Pecuch

Printed in the United States of America

ISBN 9781628392135

Library of Congress Control Number: 2012907949

www.xulonpress.com

Contents

Introduction vii

Chapter 1   Robert Herron: "The Pew Pusher" 1

Chapter 2   We Call It "Faith Webbing" 3

Chapter 3   Adelyn: A Foundation of Faith 7

Chapter 4   Elisabeth and Dawn: Making the
             Connection 10

Chapter 5   Tori: Starting From Scratch 14

Chapter 6   Whose Responsibility Is It to Spiritually
             Raise Children and Youth? 17

Chapter 7   How Does the Local Church Fit in? 21

Chapter 8   Christopher: Relying on Church Family .. 24

Chapter 9   Ryan: The Making of a Role Model 26

Chapter 10   Taylor: BFF Church Moms 29

Chapter 11   Relationship Voids 31

Chapter 12   Ashley: Filling the Gap 33

Chapter 13   Nadine: Amazing Grace 36

Chapter 14   Josh: Wrapped in Faith 38

Chapter 15   Steve: Relationships over Time 42

Chapter 16   Brittany: A Grandmother's Love 46

Chapter 17   Introducing You 50
Chapter 18   Jump Start Ideas 52
Chapter 19   Conclusion 63
About the Author 65
About the Book 67

Introduction

Officially, I have been in congregational youth ministry since the fall of 1982. When I left Philadelphia behind, I headed toward the Midwest. I arrived at St. John's Lutheran Church in Grove City, Ohio, with nothing more than a vision for youth ministry, a love for kids, and a desire to serve God.

Upon arrival, I did what was common practice at the time. I started building relationships with young people, developing a youth group, and organizing retreats and summer trips. The ministry was going well. Within a few short years, attendance was up, youth were involved, and the congregation seemed pleased.

I spent hours building relationships with students. I went to their school activities, visited them in their homes, and just "hung out" with them. I had a group of students I considered to be my core group. It was time-consuming, but I was just out of college and was willing to pour hours into the ministry.

Somewhere in the midst of "doing" youth ministry, I married. My wife, Laurie, had been a youth director, and she loved youth ministry as much as I did. Now the two of us were pouring ourselves into the youth. It seemed an ideal match for me and for the church.

After several years of marriage and ministry, however, we noticed something was missing from the youth ministry. We had great programs, wonderful retreats, and meaningful summer trips. Yet we began to notice that we weren't keeping the youth for the long haul. Youth who were very active in middle school would stop coming to events when they were in high school. Others gradually disappeared throughout their high school years. Something was missing. More accurately, someone was missing—students! And something had to change.

My wife and I put our heads together. It didn't take long to realize the youth ministry had become a program separate from the rest of the congregation. Youth knew us. But youth knew few, if any members of the congregation. Certainly, they knew their peers, but there was nothing connecting them with younger and older members of the congregation. We also noted that the youth were not involved in the life and mission of the church. If anything, they were only involved with us. Those students with whom we had significant relationships were still around, but we could only be deeply connected with a limited number of students. How could we connect more students with more members of the congregation? We had a new quest before us.

Over the years, we developed a plan to purposely connect students with younger and older members of the church. We wanted students to be aware that they were a part of the church body, to feel connected, and to be able to make a difference in the life and mission of the church. We wanted adults to recognize that students needed faith models who cared about them. We call it faith webbing.

I have been working at the same church now for over thirty years. In addition, I am currently a consultant to over two hundred congregations in the area of youth ministry. Based on my experience, I am convinced that faith webbing is the foundational concept most needed to build a comprehensive ministry to young people within a congregation.

The purpose of this book is to share with you the concept of faith webbing. We want to help you catch a glimpse of the need to connect children and youth with models of faith among all age groups within your congregation. It is an intergenerational approach to youth ministry. It's intentional and faith-based, and it works.

The stories you will be reading are all true, and yes, the names have been changed. And though there are scores of other stories we could have included, we feel these stories decidedly make the point.

Feel free to contact us if you'd like to talk more about how faith webbing can affect and improve your congregation (garypecuch.org).

> *May God weave you into the lives of others, may others draw you closer to the heart of our Lord and Savior, and may we be woven together in His love. Amen.*

> —*Gary and Laurie Pecuch*

Robert Herron: "The Pew Pusher"

His name is Robert Herron. My wife affectionately refers to him as a "pew pusher." Mr. Herron didn't actually push church pews, but every Sunday, my wife could count on him to make his way through the pews to the other side of the sanctuary just to say, "Hi."

My wife was very shy throughout junior high and even into high school, so when Mr. Herron first greeted her, she would lower her head, mumble a barely recognizable greeting, and quickly turn to avoid more conversation. But Mr. Herron was persistent. Each week, he came to her after worship, moving his way through the pews, with a big smile on his face and the words, "Good morning, Laurie. It's good to see you. I'm glad you're here."

By the time Laurie was a junior in high school, the greeting had become mutual. He occasionally still needed to "push the pews" to see her, but she was eager to say hello and often looked for him at the beginning of worship. If Mr. Herron was not in worship, he was missed.

Over the years, without either of them really knowing it, a surrogate grandfather-granddaughter relationship had been formed, and it all started with a simple greeting, "Good morning, Laurie. It's good to see you. I'm glad you're here."

What Mr. Herron did for my wife was simple. He communicated to her "I care about you," which to a young person quickly translates into "the church cares about you," and that ultimately translates to "God cares about you."

We Call It "Faith Webbing"

Our vision is to wrap children and youth in a web of faith so loving and caring that they will know Christ and always want to be a part of a local congregation. We have been developing the faith-webbing concept in our congregation for over thirty years. We started with a philosophy called "relational ministry." The goal was to have youth leaders at events that did not have programming responsibilities. These caring adults were simply present to be "relational" with young people. They were there to build friendships with children and youth with the hopes that those relationships would point youth to Christ.

Oftentimes, this relational ministry approach was a youth leader going to school functions or to community events or taking a couple of teens out to a restaurant for the sole purpose of building relationships. This relationship did prove important in the life of the young person; although sometimes it was the only significant connection to the church. If the youth leader became occupied with the busyness and demands of ministry, then the connection weakened. Worse yet, if the youth leader moved, then the connection was regrettably broken.

Faith webbing is a much deeper and more purposeful approach to connecting youth to the church. Its premise is to intentionally identify relationship voids in young peoples' lives and then fill those voids with church members of all ages. A young person is then surrounded by numerous faith walks that they can emulate. Nothing is accidental. Relationships are prayerfully, purposively, and intentional sought, built, and sustained.

The end result of this approach to ministry is that youth get to know scores of people of all ages within the congregation. They get to know these folks in a safe, fun, loving, and faith-nurturing environment. As this occurs, the church then becomes a place of deep meaningful relationships.

For some youth, there might not be a parent, grandparent, aunt, uncle, older sibling, or younger sibling in their life. In faith webbing, we deliberately identify those relational voids and then aim to fill those relationship needs with loving, caring people from within the congregation. It is common for youth to develop "grandparent relationships" with several of the older members. Thus, the church becomes a place where youth develop needed surrogate relationships.

We introduce the faith-webbing concept to children and youth in various ways. Our focus with the elementary school-aged children is on the leadership team. We explain the concept to the adult and teen leaders during training sessions. As leaders catch the vision for faith webbing, we know our children will be surrounded with lots of faith relationships. We aspire to have at least a 2:1 ratio of children to leaders at events. The leaders understand that they are there to intentionally build faith relationships with children. Together, we purposively love kids into the kingdom.

When youth get older, we offer specific faith-webbing sessions. In these sessions youth get the opportunity to begin to define their personal faith web. They contemplate who is in their faith web and who needs to be in their web. We talk about the quality traits we see in the people in their faith web. We plant the seed that youth can develop these qualities in their lives and also be in someone else's faith web. As this exercise is revisited, youth appreciate the people God has placed in their lives, they are reminded that they are not alone in their faith walk, and they are encouraged to reach out and develop more faith web relationships.

This exercise becomes a springboard for deepening relationships and a place to recognize relationship voids. Our mission jumps from sharing the vision to connecting people. We become attentive to relationship needs and prayerfully seek to weave people together in a faith-based environment. God is the supreme faith weaver. We are privileged to be the vessel through which He weaves.

Ultimately, youth become engaged with people of all ages, which leads them to becoming involved in the life and mission of the church. No longer are children and youth separated from the congregation and expected to meet with just their age group in a room set aside specifically for them, one apart from the rest of the congregation. As youth see folks in their faith web living out their faith, youth get a vision of how they can be active in serving others, often working alongside those in their faith web.

Adelyn: A Foundation of Faith

One particular occasion, we were working through the faith webbing exercise with a group of high school youth. We gave each high school student a piece of poster board and asked them to place his or her name in the middle. We then asked each student to create a web of names of people in our congregation whose faith they admired. We told them to try to list at least six grandparent-aged people, six parent-aged people, six people in their twenties, six peers, and six people younger than themselves.

It was fascinating to see their minds begin to work. Names were appearing on the papers. Webs were being created all over the room. As the writing slowed down, we encouraged students to think of their Sunday school teachers, vacation Bible school teachers, music leaders, youth group leaders, pastors, people they had heard speak at church, people they see at worship, etc.

Because we were away on a week-long event, this particular group of students worked on their faith webs a little each day. Near the end of the week, each student took a turn presenting his or her poster board to the group, sharing who was in his or her faith web and why.

Adelyn was one of the first teens to present her faith web, as she found the exercise an exciting opportunity to document her relationships. Her poster board was full of names. Adelyn shared one name and story after another. She just couldn't stop. She could have talked for thirty minutes. You see, Adelyn is one of those "church kids." She was practically born in the church. Her mom went to church. Her dad went to church. Her brother went to church. Her grandparents went to church. Her aunts, uncles, cousins, you name it, they were in church each Sunday. In addition, she had been baptized and confirmed in the church. She will likely marry in the church. Yep, Adelyn was not just a "church kid." She was a "St. John's kid."

Without knowing the concept, Adelyn had been building her web of faith her entire life. She probably had more than fifty names in her faith web, and she was still adding names as she was giving her presentation. How fun!

What's the benefit? We never had to worry about Adelyn. If Adelyn missed three weeks of church in a row, a dozen people would track her down. To her, Sunday morning was a giant family reunion where she could come and be surrounded by scores of people she loved and admired . . . and who loved and cared for her. It is a perfect faith-building scenario.

Want a greater benefit? All those years of being in the church several times a week really paid off. By the time Adelyn was a teen, she had a rock-solid foundation of faith that was unshakable. Now, as the Apostle Paul wrote in I Corinthians 3:2, she was ready to move beyond milk and get into the meatier portion of the faith. To Adelyn, seeking God's calling was second nature. What a joy it is to spend time with a spiritual teen of God!

Elisabeth and Dawn: Making the Connection

During the same exercise, at the week-long event, two other teenage girls, Elisabeth and Dawn, presented their personal webs of faith. Without the same family church ties as Adelyn, the two girls did not know quite as many people. There were gaps in their faith webs.

After the experience, Elisabeth and Dawn came up to me and said, "Gary, we don't know anyone in our congregation over fifty years of age."

"Ugh," I thought, "How tragic. The over-fifty crowd is where the wisdom is." (In fact, in our congregation we actually call our seniors the OWLs, an acronym for "older, wiser Lutherans.")

In these two girls, as in most of the youth, we noticed holes in their faith webs, segments of the congregation where they knew little or no one. Hmm, it did not take too long to figure out what the poster had become—a personal ministry plan for each student. That church experience had taken place in June. We told the teens going into the next school year that our goal and our responsibility as congregational youth leaders was to help them fill in those gaps by next Memorial Day. Yep, each student had created a one-year personal ministry plan. It was time to get to work.

Elisabeth and Dawn needed to get to know some of the older folks in our congregation, so when we returned from our trip, my wife, Laurie, invited Elisabeth and Dawn to a Saturday morning prayer group. At the time, the group consisted of a dozen or so ladies all over the age of fifty. Monthly, they sat in a circle and crocheted and knitted prayer shawls that would be given away at some point. The sound of clicking needles, conversations about life, the sharing of hopes and dreams, words of encouragement, spontaneous laughter, and moments of shared silence often filled the room during group prayer. We were confident this would be a good place for Elisabeth and Dawn. My wife connected with the group ahead of time and prepped the ladies for the visit from the teens.

The meeting went well. The ladies welcomed the girls, and the girls loved their experience. Elisabeth and Dawn wanted to come back. They did come back, and after several weeks, one of the girls caught me in the hallway.

"Gary," she said, "I love the group. I now have like seven new grandmas. This is so cool."

The girls came regularly at first and then off and on for the next four years. But imagine what went on in that group—a couple of young ladies showing up at church on Saturday mornings to "hang out" with some older, wiser Lutherans who simply wanted to make prayer shawls and love the stuffing out of a couple of teenage girls. Relationships formed; they started connecting when they saw each other at other times during the week. Simple hellos turned into longer conversations. The girls took note of these women attending worship and serving in other roles at church. Subtly and simply, faith was passed on. What great role models these wise women turned out to be to these young women. The girls had a newfound faith that was caught, not taught.

And Elisabeth and Dawn? Well, they spent the next four years perfecting their crocheting and weaving relationships.

One of them completed a prayer shawl that became a blessing to an elderly person in our congregation. The other learned to quilt. Who knows where these gifts will take them and whose lives they will touch, and that's way cool!

Tori: Starting From Scratch

Okay, but what is an example of faith webbing with a kid who isn't active in the church? For one, there's Tori. One day, my wife was at the church, and she got a call from Aunt Julie. "Laurie, you don't know this, but I'm an aunt. I have a niece that lives a thousand miles away. Her father is not a constant part of her life, and her mother just tragically died. I am about to inherit a niece. She is twelve years old, was never baptized, has not been to church much, and is about to start confirmation. I have never been a parent before, and I don't know what to do."

After some heartfelt conversation, my wife said, "Julie, start bringing her to church. We'll figure this out together."

In the meantime, we went around the church and specifically recruited eight people in the congregation to love the stuffing out of Tori. We recruited a couple of grandparent-aged, parent-aged, college-aged, and high school-aged people. We told them the sixty-second story about Tori and shared with them that a young girl who was going to start coming to our church and that she needed the loving embrace of a church family.

We asked that, whenever they saw Tori in church or around town, they specifically go up to the young woman and say, "Hi, Tori, it's good to see you. I'm glad you are here." Echoes of Robert Herron could be heard.

Over time, the greetings became longer, and conversations and relationships began to form. As Tori continued to attend church, she began to build her own web of faith. After a period of time, it was especially gratifying to see her enter the building and get a hug from Grandma Rose, Grandma Susie, and Grandpa Fred, none of whom were biologically related to her. Tori had found that the church could be a giant surrogate family to her.

After two years in the congregation, Tori was baptized and confirmed. She had developed a faith web of more than a dozen people. By the time she was a sophomore in high school, her faith web was an explosion of relationships. Throughout, she was regularly involved as a teen leader with the younger groups in our congregation, and she found herself in the faith webs of many younger individuals who now admired her faith. Tori, who had been lovingly wrapped in a web of faith, had caught the faith-webbing vision.

Whose Responsibility Is It to Spiritually Raise Children and Youth?

This directive is quite clear in the well-known passage found in Deuteronomy 6:4-9. Parents have the ultimate responsibility of spiritually raising their children. The NSRV puts it this way:

> Hear, O Israel, the Lord is our God, the Lord alone. You shall love the Lord your God with all your heart, and with all your soul, and with all your might. Keep these words that I am commanding you today in your heart. Recite them to your children and talk about them when you are at home, and when you are away, when you lie down and when you rise. Bind them as a sign on your hand, fix them as an emblem on your forehead, and write them on the doorpost of your house and on your gates.

One of the things the church does well is provide us with symbols. Go to most churches in America, and you will find symbols everywhere: crosses, seashells, flames, grapes, wheat, lamps, the Greek letters alpha and omega, candles, altars, and many more. The symbols are in stairwells, above water fountains, and in stained glass windows. You can find them in almost every room in the building. During our Holy Communion learning event, one confirmation student counted over ninety crosses just in our sanctuary. The symbols remind us of *who* we are and *whose* we are.

But how are we doing at home? The passage in Deuteronomy directs us to keep the word of God and symbols (signs of His presence) in our homes as well. Remember "on the doorpost of your house and on your gates."

My wife has placed an assortment of Christian symbols in our home. In our living room alone, there are no less than thirteen Christian symbols. They constantly remind me of *who* I am and *whose* I am. One of the symbols is a nativity scene that sits right by the television set in our living room. As I sit in my easy chair each evening and relax with the remote in hand, I channel surf to catch up on the day's events and find a bit of entertainment. Anyone who spends any time at all watching television knows that the current culture does not exactly have my personal spiritual growth as its prime directive. Inevitably, every evening, I come across images that are not in my best interest. Yes, I do have standards for entertainment and television, and I am pretty good at staying with shows that inform and entertain in appropriate ways; however, it is also easy to linger a bit on shows (or even commercials) that challenge my standards. When that occurs, I simply get a nudge by the spirit of God to glance in the direction of the little year-round crèche sitting by the TV set as He whispers in my ear, "Gary, you are better than this. Move along. Move along."

Symbols remind us to keep God first in our lives. The command to love God with all our hearts, souls, and might is so important that parents are instructed to talk about God with their children at home, away from home, and at all hours of the day and night.

So parents have the ultimate responsibility of spiritually raising their children; however, they do not have to go it alone. These days, there are many resources available to parents to help them develop a spiritual pathway for their children.

Two websites worth visiting are www.youthandfamily institute.org and www.faithink.com. Resources are great. We love resources, but even more, we love the church. Let's investigate this a little more.

How Does the Local Church Fit in?

First, there's Baptism—or maybe it is Dedication in your faith tradition. When a baby arrives, it's a wonderful time of blessings, excitement, and hope for the future. Parents want the best for their child. They wish to pass their faith on to their newborn. Yet, despite their repeated pleas, no answer is given when they ask their baby, "Do you want to be a Christian?" So parents with a spiritual orphan on their hands do the next best thing. They head to the church for Baptism.

In Baptism, parents present their child before God and officially begin the process of passing on their faith to their child. Although Baptism is so much more than what is described here, you get the basic picture. There the parents stand in a sanctuary at a baptismal fount, a pastor reading a list of responsibilities (actually *promises*) that they make before God for their son or daughter. The pastor reads the following:

Will you promise to: bring them (your son or daughter) to live among God's faithful people, bring them to the word of God and teach them about the Holy Supper, teach them the Lord's Prayer, the creeds, and the Ten Commandments, place in their hands the holy scriptures, nurture them in faith and prayer, teach them to trust God, proclaim Christ through word and deed, care for others and the world God made, and to work for justice and peace throughout the land?

Parents respond by saying, "I do."

Whoa, what a list! You can almost watch parents begin to stoop over at the enormity of the task laid before them. How can they possibly accomplish all of the above? The answer lies in why many denominations frown upon private Baptisms. The pastor goes on to say to the sponsors, godparents, and the congregation, "People of God, do you promise to support little Jasper (and his/or her parents) and pray for them as they take on these responsibilities?"

The congregation replies, "We do."

What exactly does "promise to support" mean? Remember that old Verizon commercial where the guy is talking on his cell phone, and everywhere he goes, there is an entire network of people and technicians following behind him? There are helicopters hovering overhead and commandos sliding down ropes, all there to support the Verizon customer!

That's the image I have of the congregation during the Baptism service. There is an entire network of faithful and mature Christians stating that they understand the responsibilities the parents are taking on, they know that the parents cannot do it alone in our culture today, and that they are here to help those parents. We will help teach Sunday school or vacation Bible school or become a mentor for your child during confirmation. We will sing Christmas carols alongside your son or daughter to our homebound members or serve with them at the local food pantry or soup kitchen, or we can simply take on the responsibility of earnestly praying for your child. We will help send your child on a summer church trip. We will be good examples of faith to your son or daughter. We care. And we are in this with you.

Whew, parents are comforted. The burden of responsibility is now lighter. This is doable. It takes a network. It takes a congregation. It takes faith webbing, scores of adults involved in the life of each young person. Yep, it *is* doable.

Christopher: Relying on Church Family

Christopher was a young teen helper at vacation Bible school. He was dropped off in the parking lot, except this day was a bit different than the previous day. Since Christopher had left VBS the day before, his grandfather had passed away from a long battle with cancer. Christopher's grandfather was a spiritual giant, a pillar of the congregation. Everyone knew the situation. I approached Christopher in the parking lot that morning simply to tell him that he did not need to be at VBS and that we could find someone to fill in for him. I gave him permission to leave and encouraged him to go home to spend time with his family; however, feeling the heaviness of his grief, the first place Christopher turned to was the church. He told me he needed to be at VBS; he needed to be with his church family. Immediately after he entered the building, teens and adults were offering kind words to Christopher. He was surrounded and enveloped in the love of his church family. Scores of people willing to share in his pain went to the calling hours at the funeral home, attended the memorial service, and stood beside him in the days, weeks, and months that followed.

Christopher was fortunate. Although a young teen, he had grown up in the church and had spent all of his young life developing his personal web of faith, a web that was there for him when he needed it most.

I call this concept "Early and Often." It is plain to me that most children have their flight patterns pretty much established by the age of twelve. The softball kids are softball kids. The volleyball kids are volleyball kids. The scouts are scouts. The musicians are musicians, and the 4-H kids are 4-H kids. All of which is well and good, but by age twelve, I also want them to be "church kids." They need to be; they have to be. As a parent, my goal would be to make sure my child was totally immersed in a local congregation by the age of twelve. By then, the church building would be a spiritual home, a second home, a place where young people turned to in the good times and bad.

Ryan: The Making of a Role Model

Ryan was a seventh grader when he went with us to adventure camp—a weekend experience for elementary-aged children. It's a time when the teens in our congregation get to be cabin coaches for the "little people." Each teen is assigned to "coach" one or two children for the weekend. Parents and grandparents take care of much of the programming so that the teens can focus on their relationship responsibilities.

Ryan was assigned to a six-year-old boy named Tyler. His job was to ensure that little Tyler had the time of his life at camp. The weekend took place, and the Monday morning after adventure camp, I got a call from Debbie, the mother of Tyler. "Gary," she said, "Who is this Ryan guy?"

Now, at this point, I wasn't quite sure which direction the phone call was going to go. So, with some hesitation, I said, "Well . . . Ryan is the seventh-grade coach that was assigned to your son for the weekend."

Much to my relief, Debbie proceeded to say that on the way home, all she heard from little Tyler was "Ryan did this . . . and then Ryan did that . . . and then Ryan did this." Tyler was pretty much rambling nonstop for most of the hour-ride home. She went on to say that Ryan had had a profound impact on her son that weekend. Then she asked, "Will Ryan be in church on Sunday? My son needs to see him." I told her I would do my best to see to it that Ryan was there.

So, there we were, Sunday morning in the seventh-grade Sunday school room. Class was about to start when little Tyler and his mom came to the door. Tyler's eyes were huge as he tentatively entered "the big kid room." Then he spotted Ryan. All fear left his little body, and he ran up and hugged one of Ryan's legs. Tyler had attached himself to Ryan. Ryan, nervous and not knowing what to do, repeatedly patted Tyler on the head and said, "How ya doing, little buddy?" Tyler thought Ryan walked on water. Ryan learned that day the incredible power of being a positive role model. Tyler's faith web had begun to take shape.

Fast forward. Ryan is now in college. He helps lead the middle school events he once attended as a youth. And yes, Tyler is one of the students. They have spent six years of faith mentoring together, serving at homeless shelters, going on church retreats, attending faith events, and playing basketball in the gym.

Fast forward a few more years. It is now Tyler's freshmen year in high school. Ryan watches as Tyler confirms his faith. Ryan has asked his employer if he can come late to work because he needs to attend Tyler's confirmation. Ryan wouldn't miss this for the world. Why? Because not only is Ryan in Tyler's faith web, but Tyler is now an important person in Ryan's faith web. Their faith-based relationship is mutual and enduring.

Taylor: BFF Church Moms

The Friday after Thanksgiving, Taylor and I were scheduled to meet at church to work together on a project. She was a freshman in high school. Of course, it was Black Friday, and she told me she had planned to go shopping that day and she would call me when she got back. "No problem," I told her, "Take your time and call when you get home."

Sometime, soon after 8:00 a.m., I got the call. "I'm back," said Taylor.

Because it was so early in the morning, I asked, "Back from what?"

"From shopping," she replied.

After I thought about the time frame, I said, "Oh, you didn't do that four-in-the-morning, Black Friday shopping thing, did you?"

"Oh, yeah, and I got everything I wanted," she replied. I went on to say, "God love your mom for getting up at that hour to take you Christmas shopping."

She replied, "My mom didn't take me. I went with my BFF church moms."

It turned out that two parent-aged ladies in our congregation were talking with Taylor at church when she expressed a desire to go shopping early Black Friday morning to buy presents for her parents. The two ladies simply said, "Well, if you can't find someone to take you, let us know." Taylor took them up on the offer. These two (affectionately referred to by Taylor as her "BFF church moms," BFF standing for *best friends forever*) picked up Taylor and a friend of hers early on Black Friday morning, and off they went to go Christmas shopping.

What a loving testimony to two dear adults who helped make a daughter's Christmas wish come true. As I write this today, the three of them remain close. This is what people webbed in faith do for each other.

Relationship Voids

We call them "relationship voids." Each of us has them. In my case, I grew up just north of Philadelphia. Yes, I had a mom, a dad, a brother, a couple of sisters, a few nieces, and a nephew; however, after I accepted a youth ministry position at St. John's, I found myself living in Ohio. Due to the distance, I did not see my family but once or twice a year. My closest immediate family members were five hundred miles away. I missed family in my life. The good Lord filled one void in my life by introducing me to my lovely wife, but there were still holes that needed to be filled. And if you really think about it, we all have relationship voids.

We are made in God's image. God is all about relationships. The Trinity is the perfect example of a love relationship. We need Jesus to be in relationship with God. And God knows we need each other. It's called the Body of Christ, and when it serves together, communes together, and "does life" together, it's a beautiful thing. The church was God's idea. I think God knew His people were living in a broken world and would have voids of one form or another. And in His great love, the idea was born to create the local church, a place where folks could gather and fill each other's relationship voids.

I believe we need *all* of the family relationships in our lives. We need grandpas and grandmas, aunts and uncles, brothers and sisters, cousins, and nieces and nephews. And even though I am the eldest in my family, I still need older brothers and sisters in my life. There is no greater place on earth for meeting these needs than the local church. In my congregation, I have found surrogate grandmas and grandpas, spiritual moms and dads, men I consider to be brothers, women who are as close as sisters, and of course, oodles of nieces and nephews. Once one has a healthy, developed faith web, being in the church becomes thoroughly enjoyable.

These relationships are also necessary to our faith development. That's why our faith-webbing vision is *to wrap our children and youth in a web of faith so loving and caring that our children and youth will know Christ and always want to be part of a local congregation.* Being a part of a local congregation is crucial for the faith development of our young people.

Ashley: Filling the Gap

Each year in December, our congregation goes Christmas caroling to our homebound members. One year, as a seventh grader, Ashley went along. We met at the church on a Sunday afternoon, divided into groups of about a dozen or so, practiced the first verse of a handful of carols, grabbed our route assignments, and headed off. We caroled on front porches, in living rooms, assisted-care lobbies, and people's bedrooms. We ended by praying over the folks we caroled to. It's always a powerful experience.

That day, we had finished our route and were heading back to the church. Ashley was sitting in the passenger's seat. She looked at me and said, "Gary, this was so cool. I loved it. Make sure you let me know when we go next year. I want to go again."

"No problem," I told her, "I will make sure that you know." The afternoon experience had truly touched Ashley.

Later that evening as I was sitting in my easy chair and "vegging out" in front of the television, the thought occurred to me, *Why am I waiting a year to give Ashley this type of experience again? Obviously, she was greatly impacted by the visitations. Hmm.* I touched base with Ashley and asked her if there was anyone on the Christmas-caroling route with whom she specifically felt a connection. Without hesitation she said, "John." John was an elderly gentleman who lived in an assisted-living facility. We cleared it with Ashley's family, with John's family, and with the assisted-living facility representatives. Soon, Ashley began to visit John on a weekly basis.

She visited most weeks throughout the remainder of her seventh-grade year and into eighth and ninth grade. When tenth grade came, so did the car keys, the job, and the busyness of being a high school student. Thus, her visits with John through the rest of high school were less frequent.

Then when Ashley was partway through her college career, the church received a phone call. John was not doing well. The family was not calling to have the pastor come visit. John was asking to see Ashley. We contacted Ashley, and she came to see John. The two of them had a wonderful visit as an air of closure was setting in on their relationship.

What a marvelous expression of faith their relationship had become. Soon after that visit, John passed away.

As my wife and I marveled at the years Ashley and John shared together, a thought occurred to us. Ashley did not have a biological grandfather living nearby, and John needed a young person in his life. Yet, God wove them together, fulfilling a family need they each had. God is so good!

Nadine: Amazing Grace

When Nadine was in fifth grade, she showed an interest in learning to sing the song "Amazing Grace." A woman in our congregation in her late forties who had a love for music and a love for children became aware of Nadine's desire and agreed to meet with her.

During the fall of that year, the two met multiple times to learn and practice the song. On Thanksgiving Day, near the end of the worship service, little Nadine rose from her seat and went to the top of the steps in the sanctuary. She proceeded to belt out the words to "Amazing Grace." It was fun, meaningful, a little humorous, and totally precious. What a fitting way to end a holiday service.

About a month later, Nadine's grandfather passed away. He was a long-time member of the congregation. Everyone knew him, and the sanctuary was packed for the funeral. It was a tough service as most funerals tend to be; however, none of us expected what was about to take place. At the end of the funeral, little Nadine rose from her seat and again went to the top of the steps of the sanctuary. She looked up into the heavens and began to sing "Amazing Grace."

Much different from the experience the month before, little Nadine's heartfelt rendition was powerful, spiritual, and especially moving. Imagine a little girl singing directly to her grandpa at this most poignant time. Everyone was deeply affected, and the spirit moved mightily in little Nadine that day.

Who could have imagined or foreseen the hand of God as He wove a little girl's desire and the willingness of one caring adult into such a touching moment? Faith webbing is ultimately a "God thing." It is powerful, and it is used mightily by the spirit of God.

Josh: Wrapped in Faith

Each fall the freshmen in our congregation are confirmed on Reformation Sunday, the last Sunday in October. Two weeks before, we hold our annual faith celebration. The faith celebration is an evening when the confirmation students get a chance to share their faith with friends and family.

Students begin preparing for the faith celebration in the spring. Each student is given a cardboard trifold much like you would see at a science fair. We like to call them "faith-folds." Students decorate their faith-folds based on a theme of their own choosing. Then they paste subject areas that they've written about on their faith-fold, including the following:

- A favorite Bible story, verse, or character and the reasons for choosing one.
- A narrative of a favorite service project.

- A Baptism questionnaire that one completes after he or she interviews someone who attended his or her Baptism.
- A God-sighting story in which one has seen or experienced God in his or her life or a time when he or she felt close to God.
- A personal "I Believe" statement, which one has been working on throughout confirmation.
- A representation of their faith web (one of my favorites).

On the evening of the faith celebration, the youth come and set up their faith-folds in the family life center. I meet with and prep the guests on what questions to ask the students. The guests then head over to the center. With specialty coffees or smoothies in hand, they spend the next hour walking from table to table, asking youth questions like, "Tell me about your favorite service project," or "Tell me about a time you felt close to God." The evening is followed by a Powerpoint presentation of pictures set to music showcasing the students over the years.

It's a great evening filled with faith.

You probably thought I had forgotten about Josh. I just wanted to set the stage for you. While I was going around and asking the youth about items on their faith-folds one year, I came upon Josh's faith-fold. Josh had worked on his faith-fold in class, but he had actually spent most of his time completing it at home. I was eager to see his completed project.

Josh had been going to church for all of his fourteen years of life, so he had been around. While I was perusing his faith-fold, I noticed that Josh had quite a list of names on his faith-web section. I asked Josh how many names were on his faith web, and he replied that he didn't know. We looked at the board and started counting together. The answer was seventy. I asked with surprise, "Josh, you have seventy names of people in your life whose faith you admire?"

He responded, "Oh, that's only about half of them. I just ran out of room."

Whoa, imagine being fourteen years old and having over one hundred people in your life whose faith you admire. Now that's true youth ministry. That's faith webbing to the max, and that's what our young people need in order to grow up strong and true. Can we agree that it is time to move from the old piped-piper form of youth ministry during which one or two people met exclusively with youth to try to pass on the faith?

By now, you've most likely gleaned the vision for faith webbing, but I just have to tell you about Steve.

Steve: Relationships over Time

When I first arrived at St. John's in September of 1982, Steve was one of the first young people I met. Not having any type of weekly group meetings at the time, I was searching for a way to get to know teens. Our denomination was offering a weekend event just thirty minutes away, so I figured I would try to get some youth to attend. It took an effort, but I managed to get seven girls, a female chaperone, and Steve.

Friday evening went well. There must have been two hundred teens there. Food, fun, devotions, and fellowship! It was a good evening, but then it was time for our group to split up and head to the sleeping areas. We said good night to each other. Then Steve and I soon found ourselves in a room with about eighty other guys, none of whom we knew.

So, I tried to strike up a conversation with Steve: "Where did you go to school? Do you have any siblings? How long have you been attending St. John's?" Steve, not blessed with the gift of gab, gave short, direct answers. The conversation was quickly fading. "This was going to be a long night," I thought.

I gave one final question, "So, Steve, do you have any hobbies?" Steve mentioned that he liked model trains. I simply did a follow-up statement, "Tell me about your model trains." Twenty minutes later, Steve was still talking. Yeah, I found his interest. By the time he finished talking, I knew more about model trains than any one man should. I managed, though, to stay focused and attentive throughout his sharing. Perhaps trains were growing on me!

Not many weeks after this event, I was chatting with the ushers before one of the worship services. Still rather new to the church, I was trying to get to know people and build relationships. While I was talking, I came across an usher by the name of Harold. Harold was a man in his early fifties who was a long-time churchgoer. During our conversation, the term "model trains" came up. My interest piqued. I quickly asked if he knew a young man named Steve. He replied, "Oh, yeah, he lives down the street from me." I quickly found Steve.

"Steve, meet Harold. Harold, meet Steve. You both like model trains." The two of them were off and running. I quickly backed out of the conversation.

For the next four years, anytime you wanted to find Steve, he could be found down at Harold's place. And each autumn, the two of them would pack up their train sets and travel around to the local weekend festivals. They would set up their sets on Friday evening, display them to the joy of both young and old alike, and then tear them down on Sunday afternoon. The two of them developed quite the friendship.

Now I would like to say Steve stayed involved at church all throughout his high school years because of what we were doing in the youth program at St. John's. And that may be partly true. The real reason Steve kept coming to church was because of his relationship with Harold. There's that faith webbing again. A gentleman nearly old enough to be his grandfather paid attention to him as a result of a common interest, namely model trains.

Fast forward about twenty years. I was sitting in the sanctuary on Steve's wedding day. Steve was quite the independent guy, so I had wondered if this day would ever come. Steve found himself a great woman. The big day was finally here. I was sitting next to my wife when the organ music started. The groom and groomsmen filed out from the side of the sanctuary and stood very dignified in front of the church. Much to my surprised, there was Harold, a man now in his late seventies wearing a tux. I leaned over to my wife and whispered, "What's Harold doing in a tux?"

"He's in the wedding party. He's the second best man," my wife whispered back.

"You're kidding," I said as I shook my head in disbelief. I'm not sure which surprised me more, seeing Harold in a tux or hearing that Steve had chosen Harold to be in his wedding party. As I sat there, I had to blink back tears.

Faith webbing isn't just a concept. It works. It is living, breathing, real stuff. It flows from the heart of God. It weaves us together, and it helps us stand together in all of the celebrations (and sorrows) of life.

Brittany: A Grandmother's Love

Brittany is one of those young people whose father is not a major part of her life and whose mother had to work long hours (often on Sunday mornings) in order to make ends meet. The end result was that Brittany was having a tough time getting to church.

Enter Ann, Brittany's biological grandmother. Ann is a woman with a deep faith. She wanted nothing more than to pass her faith on to her dear granddaughter.

Ann did all that she could. In fact, she went above and beyond her duties for the sake of her granddaughter's faith. Every week, Ann brought Brittany to Sunday morning worship. She went on weekend retreats, even when her legs could no longer realistically handle the rigors of the rough terrain of the church camp.

I vividly remember watching Ann struggle to walk around camp, painstakingly working her way down the long stretch to the campfire and then what seemed an endless walk back up the hill in the dark to the cabin. Ann was a trooper, all for the sake of her granddaughter's faith. And as you can imagine, Brittany adored her grandmother.

Over the years, Ann's health slowly deteriorated, and it was not too long afterward that Ann passed away. So, there was Brittany, now without her main connection to the church. What would happen to her now?

Enter Rose. Rose had no grandchildren attending our congregation. Yet, Rose could regularly be seen at church simply greeting and hugging children and teens as they entered the building for youth group events. Everyone knew Rose. Many called her Grandma Rose. Rose understood the simple concept of the *ministry of presence*. She never led programming. Oftentimes she would leave early because of the weather or the dark, as Rose was an elderly driver. Yet, she was here regularly, even weekly all though her sixties, seventies, and eighties, just showing up to greet kids with a friendly smile and a hug.

Let me retrace my steps and tell you a little about Grandma Rose. I remember one specific occasion when I was short an adult female for a week-long camping trip. I was running out of options for leaders and placed a plea in the bulletin asking for a female leader to step forward and go on the trip. Rose answered the call. At this point in her sixties, she volunteered to travel with thirty teens seven hours from home to a church camp, without many amenities in the middle of nowhere. She even participated in the hike up and over "the knob," which is actually a small mountain.

Rose did this all for the sake of loving young people and passing on the faith. Upon our return from the week-long excursion, others from her peer group marveled at her camp stories. When some of her peers suggested how great a person she was for wanting to do such experiences with young people, Rose looked them in the eye and straightened them out by saying, "No, I did not go on the trip because I wanted to. I went because there was a need." That was Rose, willing to do anything for the cause of Christ.

The first opportunity Rose had after the death of Grandma Ann, she approached Brittany and said, "Brittany, I know that your grandmother was very important to you and that you sat with your grandmother every Sunday morning in church. I could never replace your grandma, but you are welcome to sit with me during worship from now on."

Brittany took Rose up on her offer. Rose got Brittany through the tough part of those first few weeks without her grandma around. To this day, years later, it takes a group of adults working together to transport Brittany to church, weekly youth group, Bible study, and other faith-based experiences throughout the year. Well, it takes a faith web. Brittany has one. And Grandma Ann is smiling.

Introducing You

My name is (fill in the blank). Go ahead. Say it out loud. What's your name? You are a person of faith. Okay, so maybe you're not perfect. Let's be honest. Who is perfect? But by God's grace, we are His hands and feet, instruments and witnesses of His love. We get dirty, but Jesus cleanses us. We fall down, but God picks us up.

Faith webbing works not because we are these perfect people of faith but because God is at the heart and center of relationships. It's all about Him. All you need to do is be faithful and available, with your eyes on Jesus. And then live out your life, prayerfully asking God to weave you into the lives of others . . . and weave those others into your life as well.

As we strengthen and maintain these relationships with each other, we become tightly woven together as family into a web of faith.

What's the end result? Faith webbing draws us to the heart of Christ and to the church. You make a difference in the lives of others. Others touch your life in a way that is meaningful and endearing. That's pretty awesome, and we know that makes God smile!

Jump Start Ideas

Faith webbing is all about connectivity—that is, connecting children, youth, and members of all ages from within the congregation to each other. With the benefit of visiting over two hundred congregations over the years, I have been able to witness scores of congregations encouraging positive activities in order to connect their people to each other. The following pages contain a few ideas to get your mental wheels turning on how to incorporate the faith-webbing concept into your congregation.

Pew Pushers: Consider identifying those adults in your worship service(s) who have a heart for children and youth. Organize them and allow them to mingle throughout the worship area each week before the service starts, keeping in mind the objective of giving each child and teen a friendly hello. Consider having someone else track down each young person after the service to say, "It was good to see you today. Have a good week!" The goal is to greet each young person at worship service each week.

Grandparent Brigades: I visited a congregation to do a presentation on new paradigms of youth ministry. There were about forty people in attendance. Afterward, the attendees divided into groups of six to seven people. Each group was assigned the task of asking the question, "How do we make our area of responsibility within the church more youth—and family-friendly?" As I floated around from group to group, I came upon the worship team. Composed of mostly grandparent-aged people, the leader of the group informed me that they were going to form grandparent brigades, groups of grandparent-aged people who were going to stand at the door of every worship service and in her words, "love the stuffing" out of every young person who came through the door. What a great way to communicate to children and youth that they are cared about, which lets the young people know that the church and God both care about them.

The Three-Step Rule: We have a concept at our congregation called the three-step rule. In essence, when children and youth enter our building (or any room) for youth events, there will be a loving, caring person near the door to greet them before they can take three steps into the room. As those who love young people have embraced the idea, we have witnessed the joy of watching as youth enter the building and receive hugs, high fives, or simple hellos. It is even fun to watch those fourth—and fifth-grade boys "try" to get past the greeters without connecting with them. The boys seem to enjoy the attention of the chase.

Prayer Buddies: The prayer buddy system can take on different forms and can do wonders for connecting people within the congregation. Imagine the scene of a group of high school youth getting ready to depart on a summer church trip. They are in your sanctuary. Each one of them is on their knees as a preschool—or elementary-aged child is standing over them with a hand on their shoulders. Parents and siblings of the students and the children are surrounding the high school student. The pastor gives a brief word about the importance of the trip on which the high school students are about to embark. Then the pastor leads a "repeat after me" prayer that the little ones pray over the students. Everyone gives a big amen. Hugs are exchanged, and the students depart on their excursion. Once a day each day over the next week, each little prayer buddy prays specifically for his or her older prayer buddy. They say four simple one-line prayers:

> *Lord, I pray this week that my prayer buddy*
> *grows in their faith,*

earns the respect of others,
pleases you, and
then comes back to be a really good role model for me. Amen.

The high school students also pray for their little buddy each day. During travel or early in the experience, teens write a simple "thank you for praying for me" note on a postcard. The leader drops the notes in the mail as soon as they reach their destination. A small gift or stuffed animal could be given to the children at the prayer send-off or upon return. Because I have done this experience regularly for over a dozen years, I have heard many heartwarming stories. There are even prayer buddies who are now twenty-seven and seventeen years old that still keep in touch.

Prayer Buddy Variations: Okay, now get your wheels turning. *How can you incorporate a prayer buddy system in your congregation?* Maybe you can assign an adult to be a prayer buddy to each student going on the trip. You can recruit a prayer buddy for each middle school student in your congregation or for each student in a confirmation program. You can ask each Bible study group in the congregation to pray for a particular grade of students in the congregation. Set a goal that every young person in the congregation has an adult prayer buddy assigned to them within six years. Start with seventh graders and add the new seventh-grade class to the project each year. Maybe the prayer buddy system turns into a mentoring system when you ask the adult prayer buddies to meet with their students each Sunday during Advent or each Wednesday night during Lent. Or they meet with youth after significant events (a retreat, summer trip, baptism, etc.) to help them process the experience.

Faith Views: Start introducing adults or older teen members to the children and youth in your congregation. We all have faith stories worthy of admiration. Invite individuals to be interviewed in front of groups of younger individuals. Keep the interviews fairly brief, somewhere between five to ten minutes in length. Give the questions to the visitor in advance. Make it a guided interview by having someone ask the questions during the interview. Introduce the interview by saying, "This is someone in our congregation whom you need to know."

Do Speed Interviews: We have done this multiple times, always with great success. The process looks something like the steps listed below:

- Have a room set up with tables or chairs in groupings of four.

- Pair up youth and adults.

- Place pairs together (two youth and two adults).

- Give the youth twelve minutes to interview the adults. (Be sure the adults have access to the questions beforehand.)

- Consider giving the teens a clipboard and interview sheet to fill out.

- End with prayer and rotate the pairs of youth to other tables.

- Have the youth interview three or four pairs of adults within the hour.

- At the very end, mention that we are building a new culture here in the congregation. You can say, "We do not expect you to remember everyone's name. When you see each other in the future, please go out of your way to say hello to each other. It is okay (normal) to forget names, so we encourage you to start by saying, "I know we have met. Can you please remind me of your name?"

Below is a list of questions that we use during our interview times. More often than not, we cut and paste from the list to create an interview sheet specific for the event. We tend to limit the sheet to only five or six questions. Sometimes we will leave all of the questions on the sheet and ask the interviewee to choose which questions he or she wishes to answer. In all cases, we give the questions in advance to those being interviewed.

- What is your name, and how long have you been associated with our congregation?
- Why is it important for you to be involved in a church?
- Explain when and why you started attending church.
- Tell me about someone whose faith you admire.
- Name a favorite Bible story, verse, or character. Why is it your favorite?
- Share a time you felt close to God.
- Share a time that you felt distant from God.
- Share a God-sighting you recently had.
- What does your Baptism mean to you?
- What does taking Communion mean to you?
- What does Jesus's death and resurrection mean to you?
- Briefly describe your confirmation experience. If you have not been confirmed, talk about when you first came to faith.

- If you could live your middle school/high school years over again, what's one thing that you would do differently or something you would do again?

Enhancing Traditional Events: Next, let's look at programming. I am a programmer by nature, and consequently, I love programming. Programming is an essential part of congregations; however, programming is also where we spend much of our time, energy, resources, and money. Unfortunately, this process burns our people out. Before we start adding new programming to our busy schedules, I first encourage congregations to identify all of the traditional events that the congregations have on their calendars. Next, I ask the congregations to decide which events they wish to open to their entire faith community. Once decided, the question is asked of each event, "In what ways can we make the event more children-, youth-, and family-friendly?"

Church Picnics: Make your church picnic a "hobby or ministry fair." Hold your worship service outside on the day of the church picnic. Place the grills between the service area and the parking lot and ask people to stay long enough to eat and visit a couple of hobby areas. Identify hobbies of congregational members and have them host "hobby or ministry areas." The idea is to "connect" members of the congregation who have a common interest regardless of their age. Here are a few possible areas of interest:

- Prayer shawls
- Prayer warriors
- Radio Bible teaching connections
- Scrapbooking
- Gardening
- Cake decorating
- Recipe sharing
- Cookie baking
- Model trains
- Vacation travels
- Antique cars
- Automobile oil changing
- Basic car maintenance
- How to change a flat tire
- First-aid training
- New parenting
- Camping
- Fishing
- Sports (where folks can identify with others who cheer for the same teams and connect with those who have season tickets to events)

- Introductory sessions on using e-mail, Facebook, Twitter, downloading podcasts, etc. (if you have Wi-Fi)
- How to text and the meaning of common abbreviations (e.g., lol, Idk, etc.)
- Your local service ministries, your domestic ministries, and your overseas ministries

You get the picture. Once these folks connect, informal networking will begin to happen. Maybe a monthly scrapbooking group will start meeting. Maybe a church CPR class will result. Maybe parents of newborns will babysit for each other. Maybe a church fishing trip will result. This "hobby or ministry fair" can connect and weave people together.

Vacation Bible School: There is a lot that can be done around the traditional vacation Bible school to make it all church-friendly. You could do any of the following:

- Offer adult learning sessions.
- Assign relational "grandparents" to each class.
- Train teens to be helpers for classes.
- Have the oldest attendees (perhaps the sixth graders) attend a day of training to be a teen helper

and then have them spend part of a day helping in younger classes. Be sure to process the experience with them.

- Have some classes conduct an on-site or off-site service experience.

- Have teens be part of the music team.

- Ask older members of the congregation to come and be the grand marshals just for one day.

- Have a group of prayer warriors praying during the VBS meeting times.

- Ask a registered nurse to be in the building during VBS.

- Change the traditional VBS ending program to a backyard carnival with tickets, prizes, games, cakewalks, bands, bouncing houses, food, face painting, etc.

Conclusion

Faith webbing weaves children and youth into a community of believers. It builds relationships binding us together, keeping us strongly connected, and drawing us to Jesus. These faith-filled relationships fill the void and brokenness in our lives.

The more relationships, the stronger the web! We become tightly woven together. We learn together, serve together, pray together, and worship together. We reach out to each other. We walk with each other in sadness and in times of celebration. We hope together. We notice when someone is missing, and we reach out. We are never far from the loving embrace and hold of the people in our faith web.

Faith webbing is a life-long process. As youth become adults, their faith web will extend and wrap around others. It's actually a natural step in faith webbing. Inevitably, they will become the surrogate aunts, uncles, and even grandparents in faith webs of future generations.

In the meantime, our job is to be faith web designers. We partner with parents to introduce their sons and daughters to as many people of faith as possible. Together, we help to develop and grow these relationships. We share the vision of faith webbing to members of our church. We purposively program with faith webbing in mind. Ultimately, it is God who weaves our lives together. He knows us, loves us, and wants to be in relationship with us. He is the supreme faith weaver. *Thanks be to God!*

About the Author

Gary Pecuch has been the director of youth and family ministry at St. John's Lutheran Church in Grove City, Ohio, since 1982. He and his wife, Laurie, have developed a ministry for young people in their congregation based on the principle of wrapping their children and youth in a web of faith, developing faith skills in young people, and focusing on outcome-based youth ministry. Originally from the Philadelphia area, Gary has a bachelor's degree in administration of justice and a master's degree in not-for-profit administration and management. Since 2008, he has also done ministry out of his denominational bishop's office, where he holds the same title. Both he and Laurie have a great passion for passing on the Christian faith to the next generation.

About the Book

We call it faith webbing. Our vision is to wrap our children and youth in a web of faith so loving and caring that they will know Christ and always want to be a part of a local congregation. The goal is to envelop our children and youth with as many people of faith of all ages as possible—people whose faith they can look up to and admire.

It has been said that it takes a village to raise a child. From a spiritual viewpoint, it takes a congregation. That means we need a faith family in which members have an understanding of their parts in passing on the faith to our young people. Faith webbing is a concept we have been developing at St. John's since 1982. It attempts to help all members of the congregation to fill the relationship voids in each other's lives. These people are like surrogate grandmas and grandpas, moms and dads, brothers and sisters, cousins, and nieces and nephews.

In this book, you will meet various youth. Youth like Christopher, who at a young age has learned to turn to his church family in a time of need. Youth like Tori, who jumped into a congregation at the age of twelve and six years later graduated from high school totally immersed in her congregation. And you will meet youth like Josh, who at the age of fourteen has over one hundred people in his life whose faith he admires. From our standpoint, that is true youth ministry. That is faith webbing at its best, and that is what our young people need in order to grow up strong and true.

So, jump on in, meet some youth, and start thinking about how faith webbing can not only impact your children and youth but your entire congregation.

CPSIA information can be obtained
at www.ICGtesting.com
Printed in the USA
LVOW13s1119090517
533857LV00016B/311/P